A Time to Heal...

Disposing of Closet Hurts

LaShawn Myers, LCSW

Detroit, MI, USA

A Time to Heal... Disposing of Closet Hurts
Copyright © 2008, 2022 LaShawn Myers, LCSW

All scripture quotations, unless otherwise indicated, are taken from the HOLY BIBLE, KING JAMES VERSION (Authorized) and are marked (KJV).

Scripture quotations marked (NLT) are taken from the Holy Bible, New Living Translation, copyright © 1996. Used by permission of Tyndale House Publishers, Inc., Wheaton, Illinois 60189.

All rights reserved. No part of this publication may be reproduced, stored in a retrieval system, or transmitted in any form or by any means – electronic, mechanical, photocopy, recording, or any other – except for brief quotations in printed reviews, without the prior permission of the publisher.

While all of the stories and examples in this book are based on real people and events, names and identifying details have been altered to protect the privacy of the individuals involved.

*Priority*ONE Publications
P. O. Box 361332 | Grosse Pointe, MI 48236
E-mail: info@priorityonebooks.com
URL: http://www.priorityonebooks.com

ISBN 13: 978-1-933972-17-6
ISBN 10:   1-933972-17-3

Edited by Patricia A. Hicks

Cover and Interior design by PriorityONE Publications

Printed in the United States of America

This book is dedicated to
all those who want to walk in God's wholeness.

Acknowledgements

Special dedication to my mother. Thank you for the "kicks in the pants" needed to take this book off the "back burner." Thank you for all your words of encouragement and prayers of intercession. This is your time and season to be blessed. I love you so much.

Special thanks to my father. Thank you for your words of wisdom and example of strength. I love you.

Thank you Carleta for your many days of enduring the "battle" of critiquing and editing. Your patience was greatly appreciated. Much love to you.

Thank you to **All** of those who made the publishing of this book possible. I greatly appreciate and love you.

Ms. LaShawn Myers, LCSW

Table of Contents

Forewords v

Preface vii

Chapter One: Tess' Story 1

Chapter Two: What Are Closet Hurts? 5

Chapter Three: Father I Hurt 10

Chapter Four: Deliverance IS On the Way 13

Chapter Five: It's A Process 15

Chapter Six: The Enemy Comes To Steal-Maintaining Your Healing 21

Chapter Seven: Tess' Victory 33

Prayer of Healing: (My Daily Confession of Faith) 35

About the Author and Contact Information 39

Forewords

"We are hard pressed on every side, yet not crushed; we are perplexed, but not in despair; persecuted but not forsaken; struck down, but not destroyed--always carrying about in the body the dying of the Lord Jesus, that the life of Jesus may also be manifested in our body." 2 Corinthians 4:8-10(NKJV)

Most of us want to experience abundance in the newness of life but fail to simply take the time to clean out our closets in preparation for our new wardrobe. The Lord desires to clothe us in righteousness, holiness, and godliness. But before He covers us we must stand before Him naked and unashamed. God wants truth in our inmost parts. He wants to touch the places that we have hidden from others and sometimes even hidden from ourselves. However, before He clothes us with the fruit of His spirit, He cleanses us from all seen and unseen unrighteousness.

"Many people in our society are in need of healing. They have been hard pressed, perplexed, and persecuted without processing the pain. Minister LaShawn Myers calls readers to a place of true brokenness before the Lord so that He can restore the ancient ruins of abuse, abandonment, addictions, unresolved life trauma, relationship issues, grief and loss as they become more authentic in their relationships with God and others."

Many people would rather close the door on their painful past. But this text confronts the issues of sin, shame, self-esteem and much more. Minister Myers challenges others to do more than just come out of the closet but to bring with them those issues that they have tried for so long to hide.

Myers looks beyond betrayal and anger to compel the reader to process the pain, forgive and to press on through the healing power of Christ's love, restoration and reconciliation.

As an agent of change anointed with the Holy Spirit, Minister LaShawn Myers applies a healing balm to help those who long to overcome traumatic events and heal the scars left behind. With genuine care and compassion she will help you open the door to inner healing as you rid closet hurts.

Truly it is a time to heal for our youth, our elders, our leaders, and our nation. A professional clinician and minister of the Gospel, who has experienced her own deliverance, Minister LaShawn Myers is well qualified to help you through your time to heal. I highly recommend this book, "A Time to Heal – Disposing Closet Hurts" and pray that as you read it, you embrace your healing and that your life is transformed.

Rev. Dr. Sabrina D. Black,
Author, International Speaker, Counselor
Clinical Director, Abundant Life Counseling Center
Founder, Global Projects for Hope, Help and Healing
President, National Biblical Counseling Association
www.drsabrinablack.com

~ ~ ~

Timely! That's the only word that came to mind when I read Min. LaShawn's book, A Time to Heal. Amazingly, for a new author, her book is not only on time, but it's also on point. Healing in itself is no stranger to our society and to the Body of Christ. However, internal healing from what LaShawn calls "closet hurts" is. Yet, if we continue to endure this silent, compelling issue, it becomes most destructive to us because it goes far beyond the erosion of our minds, bodies and relationships to our most precious commodity, our spirits. Readers of this book will be blessed as they are enlightened on what some of those internal struggles and frustration are and more importantly, how to carefully dispose of them. I applaud LaShawn for having her pen on something so important and also what I believe is at the heart of God! For those in the Christian community, this book is a gem. Deliverance is nigh!

Rev. Dr. Debora C. Hooper
Author of Hooper's Evangelist & Minister's Handbook
Pastor, Greater Works Worship Center, Brooklyn, NY
www.DeboraHooper.com

Preface

God is the author and the finisher of your faith (Hebrews 12:2 KJV). There is nothing that has happened to you that took God by surprise. Know that our beloved God was with you even in the midst of your pain. It is through that pain that God will get the glory. How long has it been since you experienced the pain from your traumatic event? Is the pain as new as a year ago or as old as twenty? The pain from this event has caused a sense of grief and loss which leaves you feeling empty inside. You try to ignore the pain by going on with everyday life only to realize that the elephant is still standing in the room. Can you identify with the loss of a child, being in an abusive relationship, or being betrayed by a loved one (this person could be a family member or friend)? Yes, or maybe no? What life experience has caused you a sense of grief and loss? The premise of this book is to help individuals identify closet hurts (unresolved emotional and mental stress which hinders everyday functioning), to encourage individuals to seek God's purpose in pain, and finally to receive the healing that only God can provide by His love. My prayer for you as you read this book is to receive and walk in the wholeness that comes from God's healing and amazing grace.

Chapter 1

Tess' Story

"Jesus wept."
(John 11:35 - NLT)

"Beep! Beep! Beep! The annoying sound of the cell phone alarm fills the bedroom. Surrounded by fluffy pillows and warm blankets Tess fumbles to find the phone on the floor. Ughh, how did you get down there?! Picking up the phone still in a sleepy slumber, Tess focuses in enough to read the time 7:30AM. Oh no! Tess gasps, I overslept! I must have hit the snooze too many times. I have to be at work by 8:30 my boss is gonna freak! Snatching off the blankets, Tess rushes through a shower, a cold cup of coffee, and ridiculous morning traffic just to make it to work by 8:37. While punching in, Tess hears, "You're late!" Tess turns to see her boss Kathy looking over her glasses with a disapproving stare. "I apologize traffic was a little crazy…" Tess says nervously, "Save it!" Kathy abruptly interrupts. "I am in no mood for your excuses today just get to work."

Tess was viewed by others as a bright and loving person. She was known for helping anyone that crossed her path. There were times when helping others caused her to suffer lack. Tess, like most of us, has a past; a past that we keep in the closet of our mind under lock and key. There were times when circumstances (e.g. a controlling boss, overbearing family member, or a screaming child in the restaurant) would remind Tess of the pain of her past. However, she was very good at ignoring the cry of her inner voices (e.g. anger, disappointment, grief, and unforgiveness) and focusing on whatever task was before her.

Tess was the oldest of six brothers and sisters. Her best friend was her mother. The relationship between the two of them was inseparable. Often the two of them would be found sipping tea and talking until the wee hours of the morning. Tess' mother was the backbone of the family. She encouraged everyone to do their best and was a woman of great faith. She would often be found walking the floor praying or reading the Word of God when at home. The family and those who knew her viewed her as wise and strong. When Tess was thirteen, her mother was killed on her way home from work in a car accident by a drunk driver. When Tess' mother died the relationship between her and her father became estranged. The father greatly pressured Tess to fill the shoes of her mother. By the age of 14, Tess was working, going to school, taking care of her siblings, as well as the needs of the home. Tess' father greatly grieved the loss of his beloved wife. He filled his void with the consumption of drugs and women. Every other month Tess' father would introduce a new woman friend to Tess and the other siblings. The father would even allow some of the women to move into the house.

One cold late February night, Tess' father and new woman friend, who we will call Vicky, were engaging in their normal drug use. Tess was in the kitchen making school lunches for the next day while her siblings were in bed sleeping. Vicky and Tess' father were high and began to argue. The argument soon turned into a fight. They were so loud, a concerned neighbor called the police. When the police arrived on the scene, they found two adults bruised up and bloody, Tess holding and trying to comfort crying siblings, and the evidence of drug paraphernalia throughout the room. The police contacted social services and all the children were placed in foster homes. At the time of the arrest Tess was 15. Because of her age, it was difficult to find a foster home. The foster parents of the younger siblings did not want to take in a teenager. During the course of one year, Tess was placed in seven different residential facilities for girls. Unfortunately, during this time, there was no contact with her other siblings.

Around Tess' 16th birthday a foster family came forward agreeing to take her in. Tess' father was sentenced to 20 years in prison as a result of that night. Two week's after moving in with her foster family, she received a letter from the prison explaining that her father died. The prison would not allow a funeral to be conducted.

Tess' foster family was an astute Christian family. They took her to church with them and conducted a home Bible study on a regular basis. During a home Bible study, Tess asked the Lord into her heart. The foster family also worked with the agency to ensure consistent visits with Tess' siblings. Every Christmas Tess, her siblings, the foster parents, and their biological families would come together. The foster family, like her mother, would encourage Tess to do her best. They also taught her, regardless of her past, to love the Lord with all her heart. Tess graduated from high school and college with honors. Tess later became a teacher. She is currently teaching grade school math and is the youth director at her church.

Do you see yourself in Tess' story? Jesus can. Do you know the Lord is concerned about the things [closet hurts] that concern you? I believe sometimes Jesus weeps over the circumstances of our infirmities.

Chapter 2
What Are Closet Hurts?

O LORD, you have examined my heart and know everything about me.
(Psalm 139:1 - NLT)

  One would be amazed how the experiences of childhood can affect your adulthood. For example, I know of someone who finds it difficult to submit to his boss because the boss has traits which remind him of his controlling father. Someone else I know, has issues with being assertive due to a coach who belittled her during tryouts for the cheerleading team.

  I would like to talk about a concept I created entitled "closet hurts." Let me start by asking a couple of questions. First, what do we usually keep in our actual closets; items that we do not want others to see, right? Now for some of us who love to show off our walk-in clothing and shoe closets, what is done with items you don't want others to see? We place these items in the very back of the closet underneath something out of view. Closet hurts are similar because they involve unresolved thoughts and feelings usually derived from a traumatic event from childhood that are kept buried in the sub-conscience of our mental closet (i.e., one's psyche). For example, unresolved thoughts can look like; "I hate myself because I was bullied as a child and felt unloved by my parents." On the other hand, unresolved feelings can look like; "I am angry most of the time toward men because as a child I was molested by my brother and beaten by my father." The key word here is "unresolved." Unresolved denotes the incident(s) that happened which are not yet settled within our minds. One would be amazed how our minds work and how the importance of "settling" a matter impacts our mental health if not done properly. The human mind is a complex organ and needs to make sense of psychological stressors brought on by traumatic situations in life. The inability for our minds to be allotted an opportunity to properly process can have a lifetime impact. Research shows certain physical health conditions and mental health impairments originate from unresolved trauma from our past. However, be encouraged friend we will discuss in other chapters how to begin processing our "unresolved" thoughts and feelings properly. Let's keep going.

I have discovered closet hurts usually fall into two categories: (1) a hurt that is not known to others or (2) a hurt that is known to others.

A hurt that is not known to others

This category involves an experience that has caused you great mental/emotional pain and you have not told anyone about it. I counseled a youth who's grandmother was murdered while she was in the home sleeping. The perpetrator woke the child up, took her through the back door away from the home for a period of time, and then brought the child back to the home allowing her to view the grandmother in this state. The perpetrator tried to make the youth believe that the murder occurred as a result of a break in.

When I began counseling this youth, she would not speak and was very withdrawn. Her new guardian explained that the youth was naturally quiet. However, since the murder, she hardly speaks at all. As a therapist I would love to say, "Well... she talked to me." But it was quite the opposite. Initially she would not talk to me either. After six sessions of getting nowhere, we were able to discuss the event along with her feelings by drawing what happened. The young lady drew a very detailed picture of how she found her grandmother. Once this picture was drawn, the youth cried for a long time. The youth mentioned that she had never told anyone how scared she was when she initially found her grandmother lying on the floor covered in blood. She also explained that she was fearful for her life and the lives of her other siblings. Later, the guardian mentioned that the sessions gave her the courage she needed to testify against the perpetrator. The perpetrator is now serving a life sentence in prison.

A hurt that is known to others

In this category the people around you are aware of your mental/emotional pain, **but** they have no idea the extent to which the mental/emotional pain has affected you. This category can be most dangerous. Persons in this category are those who are least expected to do something out of character. For example, I knew a man who went through a divorce. His spouse of 15 years was found to be unfaithful to the marriage. Three years of counseling and being caught a second time being unfaithful (with the same person), the cheating spouse asked for a divorce.

This man was viewed by those encountered as a really nice guy. He helped others and was a community leader. He was very vocal about the details of the divorce and his feelings as a result. During the divorce hearings, he never missed a community meeting and the opportunity to help others. Several years after the divorce, he was found dating again and appeared to be doing fine. He even won an award for his involvement as a community service leader. I attended his funeral about a year ago. This man died by suicide in his home. When he was discovered, he had photos of the ex-wife surrounding him. Truly his death came as a shock to so many.

Information revealed later that during this man's childhood, his parents divorced when he was ten. During the funeral, someone recapped the man's words of loving marriage and not knowing what he would do if divorced. This man's story is an example of everyone knowing the closet hurt of his divorce, however, they did not realize the depth of his grief. His divorce brought up unresolved emotions/thoughts of his parent's divorce from his childhood. The combination of these two experiences caused him to become greatly depressed, unable to cope, therefore, taking his life.

Healing from a "closet hurt" can occur only when we first acknowledge that it happened, validate the feelings (e.g., anger, sadness, rage, shame, loneliness, disappointment, etc.) associated with the experience, and communicate the depth of that hurt to our Heavenly Father. God knows what is in your heart regarding the matter. He can heal the wounds from your negative experience. Each day as you walk this earth, the Lord is examining your heart observing the mental, emotional, and mainly spiritual damage the closet hurt has caused you.

Friend, allow God the opportunity to share His love and healing with you today.

Closet Hurt Exercise

Please take time to indicate which category your closet hurt fits in. Then write out the experience which caused your closet hurt. Also include how this closet hurt has impacted your relationship with God and other people:

_____
_____
_____
_____
_____
_____
_____
_____
_____
_____
_____
_____
_____
_____
_____
_____
_____
_____
_____
_____
_____
_____
_____
_____
_____
_____

Chapter 3
Father... I Hurt

The Lord is close to the brokenhearted; he rescues those who are crushed in spirit.
(Psalm 34:18 - NLT)

    Tess, now as an adult was doing well. She was viewed by some as "pulling herself up by her own bootstraps." Although her childhood presented much grief, loss, and disappointment, Tess was able to pull through. Tess' profession of teacher and position of youth director allotted her opportunities to mentor many youths. Tess would use the testimony of her childhood to help troubled youth overcome the trauma of present circumstances. When I met Tess, she was experiencing long periods of deep sadness. This sense of sadness would hinder her ability to concentrate at work (e.g., forgetting appointments), caused loss of interest in activities that brought pleasure (e.g., mentoring youth), and she would not go to church. I asked Tess to explain any significant changes that had occurred. Tess mentioned that she was having a reoccurring dream, which involved her talking to her deceased mother. During the conversation she remembered being happy as they shared memories. However, this man she did not know would always interrupt the conversation. Tess mentioned waking up feeling sad. Tess also mentioned that usually she could just ignore the dream and start her day. However, lately it was getting harder to let the dream go. As we continued to explore, it was discovered the man represented her father. Furthermore, her father was viewed as interfering with the close relationship Tess had with her mother.
    It was during this time that I talked to Tess about telling God, "Father I hurt." This is when you literally tell God all that is in your heart

(your feelings) and what is on your mind (your thoughts). To do this is not a sign of weakness. God wants to hear from you. It is very important during these types of experiences that we talk to God. Tell God, "Father...I hurt." Our children are a prime example of how we should communicate with God. Children, for the most part, are very trusting and honest. If they hurt, they will tell you in <u>great detail</u> all about what caused them to hurt. God is no different. He knows that he "causes everything to work together for the good of those who love God and are called according to his purpose for them" (Romans 8:28 - NLT). This experience for the greater purpose will bring you closer to Him and enable you to help others.

Tess wrote the following concerning her closet hurt:

Dear Father God,
My heart hurts today because I really miss my mom. I am also angry with my dad because he expected so much out of me after she died. Then he died in jail, I never got a chance to say good-bye. Please help me get through the feelings of anger and resentment I have toward my father. Father settle my heart as I continue to miss my mother. Thank you Father. Amen

Now it is your turn. Tell God (your Heavenly Father) all about the experience which caused your closet hurt. Cry out to Him. Tell God how this experience has made you feel. Ask God to help you cope with what has happened. God is able to heal you and help you. Give the experience and how it has affected you to God. Allow God to use this situation for His glory and purpose. Please complete the following exercise:

Father I Hurt - Exercise
Take this opportunity to tell God all about it:

Chapter 4

Deliverance IS On the Way

Wait on the Lord: be of good courage, and he shall strengthen thine heart:
wait I say, on the LORD (Psalm 27:14 - KJV)

    I purposely selected this chapter to follow "Father...I Hurt" because receiving healing is based on acknowledging that "the closet hurt" happened. Some of us, however, stop right there and just re-live the experience(s) over and over in our minds. This is keeping our closet hurt captive inside of us, which is not mentally healthy and can cause serious affects both naturally and spiritually. Mark 11:24-25 (NLT) states, "Listen to me! You can pray for anything, and if you believe, you will have it. But when you are praying, first forgive anyone you are holding a grudge against, so that your Father in heaven will forgive your sins, too." Our relationship with God is hindered when we don't forgive those who have hurt us. This issue even extends to forgiving ourselves.

    Let's stop right here, take a moment to write in the following: Father God in the Name of Jesus on (month) ___(date)___(year)____ I (write your full name)_____ forgive (list below)

1. _____

2. _____

3. _____

4. _____

It takes large amounts of energy to be angry and bitter toward someone. As you complete this list, RELEASE the person(s), no longer holding them captive in your mind. Please remember, forgiveness does not mean that you will forget what happened. Part of healing is acknowledging that the "closet hurt" occurred. How you choose to respond to this experience is what is important to recall. Use "closet hurts" to help others heal. "Yes friend, each night he beat me I hurt. But God has given me the strength to heal and help others." Or "Yes friend, it hurt me when he ran off with the money for the business deal, but God has given me the strength to trust others again." These examples display the acknowledgment of the hurt without allowing the hurt to hinder progress.

Psalm 27:14 reminds us to "wait on the Lord and he shall strengthen thine heart." In the Strong's Exhaustive Concordance the word "wait" figuratively denotes, "to expect". Ask God to help you truly forgive those that have hurt you. If this applies, ask God to help you to forgive YOU. As you do this, expect (look for) God to help you and strengthen (heal your) heart.

Chapter 5
It's a Process

And we know that God causes everything to work together for the good of those who love God and called according to his purpose for them.
(Romans 8:28 - NLT)

Well, so far we have done the following:
- Identified the closet hurt(s)
- Told God all about it
- Identified, forgave, and released those who have caused the closet hurt(s).

I hear the question, "Well, why do I still feel pain?" Don't fret my friend because that pain is all part of the healing process. We don't realize it but closet hurts often cause a sense of grief and loss (emptiness). For example, further sessions revealed that Tess was angry with her father because she had to assume an adult role during childhood when her mother died. She was also angry with her father because his lack of supervision and poor decisions caused the siblings and Tess to be placed in foster care. Tess' initial sessions revolved around not just the loss of her mother to death and siblings to foster care, but Tess also feeling the loss of her father's love because of the death of her mother.

Some of us fail to recognize the process that involves healing. Ecclesiastes 3:1 (NLT) reflects process in time, "there is a time for everything, a season for every activity under heaven" (please read verses 2-8 as well). The Webster Dictionary defines process as, "the course, steps, or methods toward a desired result." The Kubler-Ross Enumeration Stages Model (better known as the Five Stages of Grief) best describes the "course we take to [process] the desired result [to be healed from closet hurts]."

FIVE STAGES OF GRIEF
Adapted from Kubler-Ross & Kessler, 2005, p. 7-28

Stage	Definition	Closet Hurt Response
Stage #1 – Denial	Usually entails the thought of not believing the event occurred. However, not discounting the event taking place. This stage initially occurs first. According to the authors, this stage is the mind's coping mechanism. Some feelings experienced during this stage include shock and numbness.	You do not dismiss the closet hurt occurring. Your mind has decided to better cope with the hurt by telling itself, "I can't believe he/she did this to me."
Stage #2 – Anger	Anger usually involves the thought of why me?	Often I tell clients that although anger is viewed as a negative emotion it is not. What becomes the problem is the choices made as a result of the anger (e.g., choosing to kill a spouse for cheating). The authors state, "Anger is a necessary stage of the healing process. Be willing to feel your anger, even though it may seem endless" (p. 12). The Scriptures state, "Be ye angry, and sin not: let not the sun go down upon your wrath" (Ephesians 4:26 KJV).

FIVE STAGES OF GRIEF cont'd
Adapted from Kubler-Ross & Kessler, 2005, p. 7-28

Stage	Definition	Closet Hurt Response
Stage#3 - Bargaining	This stage usually involves the following questions: What if I had …? Maybe if I would have…? Sometimes you find yourself feeling a sense of mistreatment such as this circumstance is not fair. The thought is that if you had done something, then the circumstance would have changed. Guilt is a common feeling experienced during this stage. The authors state, "Guilt is often bargaining's companion. The "if onlys" cause us to find fault with ourselves and what we "think" we could have done differently" (p. 17).	I experienced the loss of a dear relationship. During this stage I found myself saying often, "Maybe if I had done something differently we would still be in the relationship." I also found myself stating, "This is not fair. I put so much into this relationship. How could he do this to me?" However, after processing through this stage I discovered I had little control over the circumstance. There was nothing I could do to change the actions of the other person. I could only change how I was feeling about it.
Stage#4 - Depression	Depression is usually experienced once the reality of the event has occurred. A common feeling experienced includes a deep sense of sadness. People usually lose interest in activities that bring pleasure. There is an attitude of not caring anymore.	The reality of the closet hurt experience has settled in. You may begin to experience a sense of loss. This sense of loss may cause great sadness. Depression is a normal part of grief. The authors state, "Depression is a way for nature to keep us protected by shutting down the nervous system so that we can adapt to something we feel we cannot handle." (P. 21). Depression experienced over extreme periods of time should involve contacting a professional mental health provider. Also during this time it is important to stay close to God in prayer.

FIVE STAGES OF GRIEF cont'd
Adapted from Kubler-Ross & Kessler, 2005, p. 7-28

Stage	Definition	Closet Hurt Response
Stage #5 - Acceptance	According to the authors this stage does not denote one being okay with what happened. However, it is being able to recognize and cope with the fact that the loss has occurred.	This stage involves acknowledgment and letting go of the past. For example, I made a conscience decision to accept the reality of my father beating me when I was a child. However, I choose not to live in the pain of that past. I also believe forgiveness plays a part in acceptance. Forgiveness in my opinion involves letting go of that person who caused the closet hurt mentally and emotionally. Not allowing him/her to control your thoughts or feelings anymore. Friend this takes time. Only God can truly help you get to this place. If you struggle with issues of forgiveness, ask God to help you. Unforgiveness holds you entirely captive (i.e., body, mind, and soul). Be free today friend and allow God to cleanse your soul.

As you find yourself going through these stages, please know that there in no exact order. Also the time frame needed to process through the stages depends upon the individual. For some individuals it may take six months to process through the stages. For others, it may take years to process through the stages. Be patient. Try not to become frustrated friend if you become stuck in a stage. If you find yourself stuck in a stage, prayerfully seek professional help.

Identifying Stages of Grief Exercise

Please take a moment to re-read the stages. List the stage or stages you are currently in. After listing the stages, briefly describe why you feel this stage applies to you. Use this exercise as a guide only. Do not take ownership of stage making it your personal friend. The idea is to identify the stage so you will know what to process through. Review your answers periodically to monitor your progress. Remember, if you find it difficult to move through a stage, prayerfully consider seeking out professional help. Please repeat this exercise as many times as needed until you reach the stage of acceptance.

Stage #1
I feel this stage applies to me because _____
_____
_____
_____

Stage #2
I feel this stage applies to me because _____
_____
_____
_____

Stage #3
I feel this stage applies to me because _____
_____
_____
_____

Stage #4
I feel this stage applies to me because _____
_____

_____

_____

Stage #5
I feel this stage applies to me because _____

_____

_____

_____

Other thoughts (please list below)

_____

_____

_____

The Scriptures state, "God causes everything to work together…" (Romans 8:28 NLT). This used to be a hard Scripture for me to read. I would say to God, "How could this closet hurt work for my good?" I believe that time has revealed God's greater purpose of lessons learned from experiences. For example the wisdom gained, the stamina developed, or the insight to help others come through similar closet hurts. The only way we are to learn the lessons from our experiences is to undergo the process. In simpler terms, instead of trying to figure out, "Why me," I began to ask God, "What do I need to learn from the experience? How can I help others who have experienced the same closet hurts?"

Chapter 6
The Enemy Comes to Steal
Maintaining Your Healing

The thief cometh not, but for to steal, and to kill, and to destroy: I am come that they [YOU] might have life, and that they [YOU] might have it more abundantly.
(John 10:10 KJV [emphasis added])

    Sometimes the greater fight is not receiving your healing but in maintaining it. Please know that the enemy will try to stop you once you are operating in your healing. The devil is very strategically subtle. The devil knows what methods to employ in order to cause you to question your healing ever taking place. For example, the enemy may employ people (usually those close to you) to remind of your past. The enemy may employ circumstances (e.g., the co-worker that always bugs you) to try to hinder your progress.

    With God's assistance it is important to become an active participant in maintaining your healing. Be willing to fight. However, when combating the enemy it must be done strategically. Consider the following five strategies:

1. Relationship
2. Stay Connected

3. Support Person
4. Professional Help
5. Journaling

Strategy #1 - Relationship
Spiritual relationship is a key element in maintaining your healing. Although the term spirituality is based on individual belief systems, for the purpose of this subject I will define spirituality as, *"one's connection with God, the Creator of the heavens and earth."* Four ways to connect with God would include:
1. Connecting with God thru Salvation
2. Connecting with God thru Scripture
3. Connecting with God thru Prayer and Fasting
4. Connecting with God thru Praise

<u>Connecting with God thru Salvation</u>

God loves you so much that He sacrificed what was special to Him, His Son Jesus (John 3:16 - NLT). In order for us to be in relationship with God, we must accept His Son, Jesus Christ as our personal Savior. To know Jesus Christ personally, we must first recognize that we are sinners separated from God and that our hope is in Jesus Christ, who came to the earth and died for our sins. We must not stop at recognizing. We also need to take steps toward confessing and turning from our sins. We must welcome Jesus Christ into our life as Lord and Savior. Please pray this prayer.

> *"Father God, I apologize for my sins. Right now, I am making the decision to turn from my sins. Father God I ask that you forgive me. Thank you for sending Jesus Christ your son to die on the cross for my sins. Jesus, I ask you to come into my life and be my Lord, Savior, and Friend. Thank You for forgiving me and giving me eternal life. In Jesus' name I pray. Amen"*

Praise God for your decision to welcome the Lord Jesus Christ as

Lord and Savior of your life. Be encouraged friend to join a Bible teaching church. This church should help you as you develop in your relationship with the Lord. Be prayerful asking God to guide you to the right church.

Connecting with God thru Scripture

      The psalmist best explained connecting with God through Scripture when he stated, "...and in his law doth he meditate day and night" (Psalm 1:2 - KJV). The term mediate in the Strong's Exhaustive Concordance denotes the word meditate as "ponder" or "study" (p.33). These two terms require time and effort. In order to connect with God one must take the time and effort to study who He is. The best way to study attributes of God is to connect with the source, His word, the Bible. The Word of God is a strategic tool to employ when maintaining your healing. There are many Scriptures to study or ponder upon concerning healing. Consider the following Scriptures:

- "Who forgiveth all thine iniquities; who healeth all thy diseases" (Psalm 103:3 - KJV).
- "For I will restore health unto thee, and I will heal thee of thy wounds, saith the LORD..." (Jeremiah 30:17 - KJV).
- " 'I have seen what they do, but I will heal them anyway! I will lead them and comfort those who mourn. Then words of praise will be on their lips. May they have peace, both near and far, for I will heal them all,' says the LORD" (Isaiah 57:18-19 - NLT).
- "You heard their cries for help and saved them. They put their trust in you and were never disappointed" (Psalm 22:5 - NLT).
- "The Lord is close to the broken hearted; he rescues those who are crushed in spirit" (Psalm 34:18 - NLT).
- "There is a time for everything...a time to heal" (Ecclesiastes 3:1, 3 - NLT).

Connecting with God thru Prayer and Fasting

      Prayer means to simply talk with God. Other than acknowledging and respecting His Holy nature (Luke 11: 1-4 and 1 Peter 1:16) there is no precise wording to use when talking with God. Remember that your conversation with God should not be one sided where you are doing all the talking. Quiet yourself so that you can hear God when He speaks back to you. Quieting yourself should be taken in the literal sense. Take some time out of your busy schedule and find a quiet place (e.g., your bedroom, your den, your car, the park, or the library) to hear from God. God speaks often in a small still voice to the quiet place of our soul. This lesson is learned from the prophet Elijah (1 Kings 19). He was faced with adversity when Jezebel sent word that she was going to kill him. Distressed Elijah began to talk with God about the situation. Observe the following verses:

> *"And he [Elijah] said, I have been very jealous for the Lord God of hosts: for the children of Israel have forsaken thy covenant, thrown down thine altars, and slain [killed] thy prophets with the sword; and I, even I only, am left; and they seek my life, to take it away. And he [the LORD] said, Go forth, and stand upon the mount [mountain] before the LORD. And, behold, the LORD passed by, and a great and strong wind rent [tore] the mountains, and brake in pieces the rocks before the LORD; but the Lord was not in the wind; and after the wind an earthquake; but the Lord was not in the earthquake: And after the earthquake a fire; but the LORD was not in the fire: and after the fire a still small voice"* [vss. 10-12 - KJV emphasis added].
>
> *"When Elijah heard it, he wrapped his face in his cloak and went out and stood at the entrance of the cave. And a voice said, 'What are you doing here Elijah?' "* (vs 13 NLT).

Here you can see the communication between God and Elijah. Elijah talks to God about his circumstance and God responds by asking him to meet Him on the mountain (vs 11) and asking the question, "What are you doing here Elijah?" (vs 13).

Fasting is another way to connect with God. It is going without... so that one can concentrate on God instead of worldly things. The purpose of fasting is not to change God's mind about your circumstance. Nor is fasting meant to answer the gnawing question of, "God, why did you let this closet hurt happen to me?" Fasting places you in a position to hear and receive from God on how to maintain your healing. Let's consider the story of King Jehoshaphat found in 2 Chronicles 20. King Jehoshaphat was faced with some disturbing news that the armies of the Moabites, Ammonites, and others decided to start a war with him. Please review the following verses:

(vs 3) "And Jehoshaphat feared, and set himself to **seek the Lord**, and proclaimed a **fast** throughout all Judah."

(vs 4) "And Judah gathered themselves together, **to ask help of the Lord**; even out of all the cities of Judah they came to seek the Lord."

Notice here that Jehoshaphat is not seeking God to find out the purpose of the request for war, but to inquire of God for direction. Let's look a little further...

After a short prayer by King Jehoshaphat (2 Chronicles 20:6-12), God sent an answer through Jahaziel the son of Zechariah. He said,

> "Listen, King Jehoshaphat! Listen, all you people of Judah and Jerusalem! This is what the Lord says: Do not be afraid! Don't be discouraged by this mighty army, for the battle in not yours, but God's. Tomorrow, march out against them. You will find them coming up through the ascent of Ziz at the end of the valley that opens into the wilderness of Jeruel. But you will not even need to fight. Take your positions; then stand still and watch the Lord's victory. He is with you, O people of Judah and Jerusalem. Do not be afraid or discouraged. Go out there tomorrow, for the Lord is with you!"
>
> (2 Chronicles 20:15-17 - NLT).

Wow! Look at how powerful prayer coupled with fasting is! King Jehoshaphat communicated to God the need for instruction. The fast positioned the King and the people involved to hear God's instruction which was spoken through Jahaziel. God can choose any person or circumstance to send direction. Therefore, we must be open to receive from God even if it is through someone we least expect (i.e., your enemy, a child, your least favorite minister at church, etc.).

I can hear your thoughts friend, "Okay, so what do these stories have to do with me?" Your circumstance is the enemy coming to distract you from the fact that God has healed your heart from the closet hurt(s). Remember only you know what those distractions can be (e.g., family members, co-workers, children, person in the grocery line, etc.).

Identifying Distractions Exercise
Please take a moment to list your possible distractions:

1. _____

2. _____

3. _____

4. _____

5. _____

Choose a day (or days) to fast (refraining from food and/or a favorite activity, e.g., watching TV or talking on the phone). Substitute the time used during your favorite activity to communicate to God about His direction on how to combat the enemy in order to maintain your healing. Remember prayer (communicating with God) involves two parties (after talking to God, listen for God to speak). Make sure you have a journal or a digital recorder handy. Write down whatever you hear God speak to your heart either during your quiet time, through people (be open, the answer may come from an unexpected person), or a circumstance. Please repeat this step as often times as needed.

Connecting with God thru Praise

"I will bless the Lord at all times: his praise shall continually [even during times when the fact of my healing is being challenged] be in my mouth (Psalm 34:1 - KJV [emphasis added]). Easier said than done huh? I have found praising God in times of challenge may not move the situation but instead it brings a sense of peace. There is something about this peace which gives the strength to move forward. Consider this, "Don't worry about anything; instead, pray about everything. Tell God what you need, thank Him (praise Him) for all He has done. If you do this, you will experience God's peace, which is far more wonderful than the human mind can understand. His peace will guard your hearts and minds as you live in Christ Jesus" (Philippians 4:6-7 - NLT [emphasis added]). As you praise God and thank Him for how He has healed you from the closet hurt(s), let Him guide and comfort you.

Finally, when the enemy comes to distract you from the fact you are healed, connecting with God through praise should be employed. Let's look again at King Jehoshaphat's example. After the king received his direction from God through Jahaziel, the King and the people bowed down to the ground worshiping God. The Levites (equivalent to ministers of today) stood to praise the Lord with a very loud shout (2 Chronicles 20:18-19 [emphasis added]). Let's pause here for a moment. You do not have to be a minister or leader of any sort to praise God.

Praise Break Exercise

Please take a moment to find a place where you can give a shout out to the Lord thanking Him for what He has done in your life. Just let go. Ready...Set...Go! Take a moment to write down how you feel after doing so.

_____

_____

_____

_____

_____

_____

_____

_____

Now that we have completed our praise break, let's finish the point of the story shall we?

The Scripture continues, "After consulting the leaders of the people, the king (Jehoshaphat) appointed singers to walk ahead of the army, singing to the LORD and praising him for his holy splendor. This is what they sang: 'Give thanks to the LORD; his faithful love endures forever!' [PLEASE READ THE NEXT PASSAGE CLOSELY] At the **moment they began to sing and give praise,** the LORD caused the armies of Ammon, Moab, and Mount Seir to start <u>fighting among themselves</u>. The armies of Moab and Ammon turned against their allies from Mount Seir and killed every one of them. After they had finished off the army of Seir, they turned on each other. So when the army of Judah arrived at the lookout point in the wilderness, there were dead bodies lying on the ground for as far as they could see. **Not a single one of the enemy had escaped"** (2 Chronicles 20:21-24 - NLT [emphasis added]). Please note friend that their praise did not cause them to escape the challenge of facing the enemy. However, look how God's peace was manifested: they did not have to fight at all.

I want to encourage you friend to employ praise when your facing the challenge of maintaining your healing. Even if you don't want to, continue to praise God anyway. Listen to music that will encourage you to praise God. Get creative, develop your own praise song unto the Lord.

Write A Song to The Lord Exercise

Provided in the space below develop a song. Now I can hear your thoughts, "Uh Sister LaShawn I cannot sing." NO MATTER! Sing to the Lord a new song ...and sing with joy (Psalm 33:3).

_____
_____
_____
_____
_____
_____
_____
_____
_____
_____
_____
_____
_____

Another technique to employ when praising God includes dancing. Now friend stop laughing. I can hear your thoughts, "I can't dance any more than I can sing". Remember friend God is looking at your heart not necessarily your ability to exhibit perfect rhythm and pitch. As with singing, find a song which will encourage you to praise God through dance. Just began to wave your hands up high, spin, smile, bow and dance into the presence of God.

Strategy #2 Stay Connected
When trying to maintain your healing, you must stay connected with people that can help you stay focused. The Word of God states, "Not forsaking the assembling of ourselves together, as the manner of some is; but exhorting one another: and so much the more..." (Hebrews 10:25 - KJV). There is safety in numbers. The church community can serve as a support when you are working to maintain your healing. Prayerfully connect yourself to a Bible teaching church which supports the healing and deliverance ministry.

Strategy #3 Support Person
Your support person should be someone you trust; preferably a family member, close friend, church member, or maybe a co-worker. This person should be someone you know will not share your information with others. It is essential for this person to be someone who is prayerful, wise, and is in relationship with God. These types of people, because of their love for God, should only want God's will for your life TO MAINTAIN YOUR HEALING. Therefore, when situations arise to challenge maintaining your healing, this person instead of being carnal in the situation (e.g., "This is what I think. If I were you...") will be supportive (e.g., "What did God say?").

Identify Support Person Exercise
List below your support person and why you selected them.

My support person is:

_____

This person is my support person because: _____

_____
_____
_____
_____

Strategy #4 Professional Help

    I know this strategy can be hard to stomach for some us. I have heard people say, "We don't air our dirty laundry," or "What is said (or done) in this house stays in this house." However, there are times when professional help should be employed. The Word of God states, "The earth is the LORD's, and everything in it. The world and **all its people belong to him**" (Psalm 24:1 - NLT). As with doctors or any other professional, God has gifted individuals to become therapists, counselors, psychiatrists, and psychologists. I would suggest that the chosen mental health provider be someone that can provide services from a faith-based standpoint. It is my belief that mental health services are best employed when therapeutic approach is combined with the Word of God.

Strategy #5 Journaling

    Journaling can be cleaning for the soul. Usually I use journaling to write letters to God about what I am thinking or feeling. I also record what God speaks to my heart (e.g., a Scripture or a song). Instead of writing, some people will utilize journaling to draw their thoughts and feelings. Journaling can help you monitor your progresses as well as set backs. Yes, I said, setbacks. Please know friend that there might be days where you might have a setback. If you do, get back up and with God's help start again. Remember, "...despite all these things, overwhelming victory is ours through Christ, who loved us" (Romans 8:37 - NLT).

Journal Exercise

Please take a moment to journal (write or draw) your thoughts down concerning you maintaining your healing.

Date:

It is important that you implement your strategies 1 thru 5 frequently. Some strategies may need to be used more than once.

Chapter 7

Tess' Victory

"...in all these things we are more than conquerors through him that loved us".
Romans 8:37 KJV

Tess made impeccable progress. After months of intervention, Tess is doing much better mentally, emotionally, and spiritually. Tess was able to describe to God in detail the places she hurt. With much work she was able to forgive and release her father. Tess continues to teach and mentor youth through her church community. Tess is a living example of the Romans 8:37 in all things (i.e., mother dying, dad's withdrawal of love, separation from siblings being placed in foster care, and processing out her closet hurts), Tess is a conqueror. Tess, with the help of the Lord, became more than her closet hurt.

We no longer have to wait to receive healing. God "is able to do exceeding abundantly above all that we ask or think, according to the power that worketh in us" (Ephesians 3:20 - KJV). God can heal every wound, water every dry place, wipe every tear, fill every empty place, and bring victory. Victory in your mind! Victory in your soul! Providing a peace which passeth all understanding keeping your heart and mind through Christ Jesus (Philippians 4:7 KJV). Ask God today to help you. Be willing to go through the process that is necessary for you to be totally healed and feel fulfilled. Then help someone else in their time of need. God is forever faithful.

Victory Exercise

Please journal (write or draw a picture) of the progress you made as a result of reading this book.

Prayer of Healing
(My Daily Confession of Faith)

"Life and death are in the power of your tongue…" (your speech) (Proverbs 18:21 - KJV). We are snared by the words that come out of our mouth (Proverbs 6:2). These are two powerful Scriptures that remind us the importance of watching what we say. Again we must take an active role in maintaining our healing. Please take the time to read this prayer daily until you commit it to memory.

Prayer

Father God, I come to You as Your Word states in Hebrews 4:13 naked and open. I give to You every closet hurt that I spoke about throughout this book and any other closet hurt that might arise in the future. I thank You for being the author and finisher of my faith (Hebrews 12:2). For making the crooked way straight (Luke 3:5) concerning negative emotions and thoughts that I might foster. Be my helper to maintain my healing, implementing strategies wisely, and assisting others in doing the same. Not my will Father but Your will be done in earth as it is in heaven (Matthew 6:10) concerning my fate. I decree and declare that I AM HEALED OF EVERY CLOSET HURT. Thank You Father God for calling me beloved (Colossians 3:12) and friend (John 15:15). Thank You for healing my heart and mind of past and possible future closet hurts. Regardless of the circumstance I know that You are allowing it for Your purpose and for my good (Romans 8:28). I love You Father God. In Jesus' name, Amen.

Don't just stop here. Let's complete one final exercise. Create your very own Prayer of healing. Remember to incorporate Bible verses with the prayer.

Final Exercise
My Prayer of Healing

References

Blue Letter Bible. 1996-2008. 17 Oct 2008. < http://cf.blueletterbible.org/lang/lexicon/lexicon.cfm?Strongs=H06960&t=kjv >

Kessler, David., and Kubler-Ross Elizabeth. 2005. *On Grief and Grieving Finding the Meaning of Grief Through the Five Stages of Loss*. New York: Scribner.

Kings James Version Bible

New Living Translation Bible, Living Water Edition. 1996. Wheaton, IL: Tyndale House Publishers, Inc.

Nichols, V. 1993. *Webster's Two in One Dictionary and Thesaurus*. United States of America: Nickel Press.

Strong, James. 1995. *The New Strong's Exhaustive Concordance of the Bible*. Comfort Print Edition. Nashville, TN: Thomas Nelson, Inc.

About the Author

Minister LaShawn Myers, LCSW, is a native of Detroit, Michigan. She has been providing service to God's people for over twenty years through teaching, preaching, counseling, praying, praise dancing, developing programs, and encouragement.

In 2002 she received her Masters of Social Work degree from Wayne State University specializing in cognitive-behavioral therapy. Minister Myers is a Licensed Clinical Social Worker with the State of Michigan. and is the founder of Great Futures Family Services, Inc., a 501 (C) (3) nonprofit organization that provides assistance to low-income pregnant women and families with children 0 to 3 through home visitations and wellness groups. Great Futures mission is to strengthen families and produce positive outcomes for families in low-income communities.

Minister Myers is currently the CEO of TheH3Network, PLLC. TheH3Network provides adults and children a safe space to discuss issues which are causing emotional or mental stress. Ms. Myers, LCSW provides coaching and consultation that assists individuals in addressing general conflict. TheH3Network also offers virtual or in-person fun, interactive, wellness workshops to businesses, nonprofits, schools, and churches.

She is a member of Merciful Ministries Church International in Redford, Michigan.

Contact Information

Ms. LaShawn Myers, LCSW can be reached for consultation appointments or speaking engagements by the following:

Phone/Text: (248) 657-3818

Fax: (586) 200-3885

Email: TheH3Network@gmail.com

DM on Social Media: www.facebook.com/TheH3Network

BOOK ORDER FORM

A Time to Heal:
Disposing of Closet Hurts
By LaShawn Myers, LCSW

Name _____

Address _____

City _____ State _____ Zip _____

Phone _____ Fax _____

Email _____

Quantity	
Price (each)	$10.99
Subtotal	
S & H (each)	$2.99
MI Tax 6%	
TOTAL	

METHOD OF PAYMENT:
*Check or Money Order:
Make payable to: **LaShawn Myers**
(in memo section please write; Book, A Time To Heal)

Credit Card:
Payments are process through PayPal only at **www.paypal/LMyersLCSW**

Cash App: **$LMyers77**
(In "For" section please type: Book, A Time To Heal)

Zelle: Call (248) 657-3818

Mail your payment with this form to:
Ms. LaShawn Myers
c/o TheH3Network, PLLC
15892 Orchard Lane | Roseville, MI. 48066 | (248) 657-3818
Email: theh3network@gmail.com

www.ingramcontent.com/pod-product-compliance
Lightning Source LLC
Chambersburg PA
CBHW052043070526
44584CB00018B/2587